Charles Ira Bushnell, Tarleton Brown

Memoirs of Tarleton Brown

A Captain of the revolutionary Army

Charles Ira Bushnell, Tarleton Brown

Memoirs of Tarleton Brown
A Captain of the revolutionary Army

ISBN/EAN: 9783337153595

Printed in Europe, USA, Canada, Australia, Japan

Cover: Foto ©ninafisch / pixelio.de

More available books at **www.hansebooks.com**

MEMOIRS

OF

TARLETON BROWN,

A

CAPTAIN IN THE REVOLUTIONARY ARMY,

Written by Himself,

WITH

A PREFACE AND NOTES.

BY

CHARLES I. BUSHNELL.

NEW YORK:
PRIVATELY PRINTED.
1862.

PREFACE.

NO where has there been so little contributed to the literature of American Revolutionary History, as in the Southern States. The deeds of Southern patriots, their valor and their sufferings, have been but little credited, because they have been but little known. While almost every Northern town has had its historian, and almost every Northern hero has had some one to perpetuate his memory, the South, though equally worthy of attention, has had, unfortunately, but few chroniclers. Her writers have been limited, her historians few and far apart.

The little that has appeared, is eminently worthy of attention, and its value to the historian is greatly enhanced, from the fact of its scanty representation in the common stock. Every effort ought, therefore, to be made, not only to preserve what has already appeared, but to add, as far as lies in our power, to the store.

It is with these views, and to further these objects, that we present the following narrative. Appearing originally in 1843, in the Charleston Rambler, a paper of limited circulation, it would, in the usual course of events, soon have become extinct. In fact, even at the present time it would be almost impossible to procure a copy. We have therefore determined to reprint it, and it is accordingly presented in the present form, with the addition of many historical notes and biographical notices.

The author was a respectable inhabitant, for many years, of Barnwell District, S. C., and enjoyed the respect and esteem of all who knew him. He died in the year 1846, at the age of 92 years.

INTRODUCTION.

BEING persuaded that a few hints in relation to the scenes in which I bore a part, in that glorious and memorable struggle for independence, which has signalized us among the nations of the earth, would not be unacceptable to my friends and the general reader, I have precipitately thrown together the following facts, which are submitted without further comment.

MEMOIRS.

Y father, William Brown, was a planter in Albemarle county, Virginia, where I was born on the 5th day of April, 1757.— Flattering inducements being held forth to settlers in the rich region of South Carolina, contiguous to the Savannah river; and my uncle, Bartlet Brown, having already moved, and settled himself two miles above Matthew's Bluff, on the Savannah river; my father brought out some negroes, and left them with his brother to make a crop; and in 1769, a year afterwards, my father and family, consisting of eleven persons, emigrated to this country and settled on Brier's

Creek, opposite to Berton's ferry. We found the country, in the vicinity, very thinly inhabited. Our own shelter for several weeks, to protect us from the weather, was a bark tent, which served for our use until we could erect a rude dwelling of logs.

Having cleared a piece of land, we planted, and found the soil to be exceedingly fertile in the river swamp, producing abundant crops. The country was literally infested with wild beasts, which were very annoying to the inhabitants; killing the stock and destroying the crops; and were so bold, daring and ravenous, that they would come into our yards, and before our doors, take our sheep and poultry. Indeed, it was dangerous to venture out at night, beyond the precincts of our yards, unarmed. We used every device to exterminate them, and ultimately effected our object by setting traps and poisoned bait.

The forest abounded with all kinds of game, particularly deer and turkeys—the former were almost as gentle as cattle. I have seen fifty together, in a day's ride in the woods. The latter were innumerable, and so very fat, that I have often run them down on horseback. The range for cattle was excellent; it was a very common thing to see two hundred in a gang in the large ponds. In any month in the year, beeves in the finest order for butchering, might be obtained from the forest. It was customary then to have large pens or enclosures, for cattle under the particular charge or direction of some person or persons. I was informed by one of those who kept a pen at King Creek, that there had been marked that spring seven hundred calves. Our produce for market was beef, pork, staves, and shingles. There was but little corn planted in that section then; and indeed there was scarcely any inducement to plant more than sufficed for our own consumption, there being but few mills in the country, and consequently very little demand for the article.

From the fact of the new and unsettled state of the country, it may readily be inferred that the roads were very inferior; in truth they were not much better than common bridle paths; and I feel confident in asserting that there were not, in the whole Barnwell District, any conveyances superior to carts of common wood slides. There were a great many wild horses running at large in the forest when we first settled in the district, a number of which were caught and sold by various individuals, who pursued exclusively, the business for a livelihood.

In 1775 the war broke out in South Carolina, and troops were required for the service—a draft was accordingly ordered in our section, and being one among the drawn number, we forthwith took up the line of march for Pocotaligo, then under command of General Bull, where we were stationed about seven weeks. Nothing of importance requiring our attendance at that place, our company was discharged, and we returned to our homes, where we had scarcely arrived, when another draft was ordered, for the first siege of Savannah, Georgia. On this occasion I escaped being drawn, but was employed by William Bryant to act in his place.

We embarked in an open boat, on the Savannah river, Capt. Moore commanding our company. After three days' passage down the river we arrived at Savannah, in good health and in fine spirits, all eager to engage in the contest, and to assert our rights as freemen through the muzzles of our muskets, and at the points of our swords. We passed some heavy and mortal shots at the enemy, which were returned with equal fierceness and more deadly effect. During the heat of the battle, the iron hail pouring in torrents upon our devoted heads, a ball struck me in the breast, but being well nigh spent, it providentially did no other damage than raise a blood blister. We stayed at Savannah about seven weeks, and then returned to South Carolina, under the command of Gen. Bull. (1)

Having now become greatly attached to the army, in April, 1776, I enlisted in the regular service at Fort Littleton, Beaufort District, commanded by that brave and sagacious officer, Capt. William Harden. (2). There were about eighty-five men stationed at Fort Littleton, and I am the only one now remaining of that number. The greater part of the rest, through the fortunes of war, left their bones bleaching upon the battle plains ; the few who survived the ravages of war, have long since fallen beneath the cold and relentless hand of death.

In July, 1777, I left Capt. Harden, but immediately joined Col. James Thompson's detachment on Pipe Creek. While stationed there, I accompanied Capt. John Mumford, and a few choice fellows, upon an expedition to Georgia, to take a guard commanded by Capt. Mott, a tory, near Hutson's Ferry. We thought to surprise them ; but, through some unaccountable means, they had discovered our intentions some time before we reached the house where they were barricaded, and snugly encasing themselves, were prepared for our attack, and kept us at bay by firing at us through their port holes. The enemy, from their favorable position, could single out our men with deadly aim.

During the engagement, I screaned myself behind a tree, with the two fold object of protecting myself from danger and taking deliberate aim at the enemy. Whilst in the act of shooting, a ball from the fort struck the tree just above my head, and dashed the bark into my face. I was rather cautious how I projected my head again beyond the necessary limits. As our captain was now severely wounded in the knee, and John Booth mortally, of which he soon died, we gathered our wounded in blankets, and returned to South Carolina, to Col. Thompson's camps. When Charleston fell into the hands of the British, under the command of Sir Henry Clinton (3) and Admiral Arbuthnot, (4) Captain Mumford, in attempting to make his way to the American Army, was attacked at Morris's Ford, Saltketchie, by old Ben John, and his gang of tories. In this encounter, the poor fellow lost his life, and a truer patriot and braver soldier never fell. He now sleeps at the foot of a large pine, on the left hand side of the main road to Barnwell C. H., a few rods south of the bridge, just at the turn of the road from which you can see the bridge.

SIR HENRY CLINTON

A short time after these misfortunes, being stung to the quick at our recent defeat and irretrievable loss, and thirsting for justice, a company of fifty horse, led on by Col. Thompson and Major Bourguoin, sallied forth on a second expedition to take the formidable Captain Mott and his allies. In this instance, fortune favored us. I took part of the company, and went between the house and swamp. Our approach was so quiet and unexpected by the tories that, making a charge upon them, they, without the least effort to defend themselves, surrendered. Taking our prisoners, we returned in triumph to our headquarters, and from thence they were sent to Charleston under a strong guard.

After this capture of Capt. Mott, and his band of tories, I continued with Capt. Thompson but a short time. Leaving him in conjunction with Joshua Inman and John Green, I raised a company of horse, which we called the "Rangers," with the view of scouting those sections of the country adjacent to the Savannah River, both in Georgia and Carolina, as occasion required. Our station was at Cracker's Neck, S. C. Whilst there, our rude boys would go out in the back swamp, and frolic with the inhabitants, and from the great quantity of pinders they saw among them, said they would give it the name of Pinder Town, by which name it has gone ever since, as it is now well known by the name of "Pinder Town." During our stay at Cracker's Neck, we took two trips to Sunsburry, Midway Settlement, Georgia, under the command of Generals Pickens, (5), and Twiggs. We had a fight with the British and tories on Ogeechee Causeway; but not much damage was sustained on either side.

In one of our trips to Midway, a young man by the name of Richardson went ahead of us for the purpose of advising the enemy of our approach, but there lived a Mr. Cooper upon the road, directly in our route, who had a pretty daughter named Jane; and it was well known that young Richardson was in love with Miss Jane, and we suspected that he would call in to see her, so I selected a few men, and by a shorter way between the house and the swamp, intercepted him. He was, as we conjectured, at Cooper's, and as soon as he heard the approach of our men, he ran out—we fired upon him, and left him dead. Cooper ran through an old field, but we sent a few shots after him, one of which entered his heel and stopped him, (I think the distance was nearly two hundred yards)—we brought him to the house, and left him with his family.

In our two trips to Georgia, we made a road in it, which since has become a public road, and is now called the "Rebel Road." Georgia, at this time, was completely in the hands of the British and tories. They often crossed the river, and killed and plundered the Whigs without mercy. On one occasion, I visited my father and the family, with the view of remaining with them all night. On arriving at home, I was pleased to find my brother-in-law, John Joice, and a friend from Augusta there, on a visit for a short time, for the times were now dangerous, the tories having threatened my life and the life of one of my brothers. I felt that in case we were attacked they might render us essential service. And it so came to pass that on this very night they came to put into execution their threat. It was about midnight when they arrived. I was sleeping in the hall, and was awakened by the barking of the dogs. In a few moments I was brought to my feet by a loud rap at the door :—I asked, "Who's there?" Several voices together replied "friends," and said that they were from Sister's Ferry, (6) Gen. Lincoln's (7) army— that their term of enlistment had expired, and that they were now on their return home—were greatly fatigued from traveling, and would like to remain with us during the night. I expressed to them my regret at our inability to accommodate them, as our house was filled with company. After a few minutes' secret deliberation, they asked for a torch of fire, and said they would go to Brier's Creek (8) and encamp. I felt disposed to accommodate them as far as practicable, yet I had some misgivings with regard to the truth of the statement they had made, but recollecting that the militia were about to be discharged at that point, my doubts were in a great measure removed. I therefore opened the door and handed them a light, but, as if directed by a supernatural agency, I instantly closed it again, and looking through the crack above the door, I could distinctly see what passed among my friends without, by the light of their torch, and to my astonishment I found them to be tories. Here judge of the narrow escape I made. With what ease could they have put an end to my existence, entered our abode and massacred all within, ere we could have been aroused to a sense of our danger, Coming to the door a second time, they asked for water. I had now discovered the true object of their mission, and was upon my guard. Having made the door doubly fast, I told them in a repulsive tone they might get it out of the well in the yard. This exasperated them exceedingly, and with loud voices they denounced me, father, and all the family, threatening to visit vengeance upon the whole household, and with fiendish fury and united strength, endeavored to burst the door from its hinges, but finding they could not, they endeavored to shoot me through the crack, (it being a log house, as before mentioned) and they had a tolerable fair chance to do so, as the door of the room in which my father and the family lay was open, and the light shining through it from the room into the hall where I was. They fired four or five times, but missed me and killed my little brother, who was aroused by the uproar. By this time we had gathered our arms, and they made off some little distance from the house, still firing, but to no effect. We were well supplied with powder and ball, and if they had been men and stood their ground like soldiers, (and not have skulked off into the dark as all cowards and villains do when there is an opportunity offered to fight on equal grounds) we would soon have given them what they richly deserved. I have good reason to be thankful to Almighty God for his kind care and protection of me through so many dangers. I can plainly discern a divine interposition in my deliverance from the hands of those prowling murderers and plunderers.

A few months subsequent to this period, I withdrew from the "Rangers" at Cracker's Neck, and connected myself with a company of militia keeping guard at Burton's Ferry. We exchanged shots almost every day with the British and tories, who were on the opposite side, (Georgia.) A man moved over and joined our party, who said he had buried three jugs of rum at Hershman's Lake, and designated the spot. One of our number (Benjamin Green) said he knew the place, having once lived in the vicinity of the lake,—so being in the right humor for an exploit, we soon devised, and put into execution, a plan for visiting the premises. Benjamin Green, Henry Best, John Colding, and myself, took a small canoe, and proceeded down King Creek to Savannah River; while we were moving up the stream of the river, with every prospect of success in our enterprise, a gang of tories, numbering thirty-five, suddenly appeared upon the bank, where they had been lying in ambush awaiting our approach. They hailed us, swearing that if we did not come to and surrender they would kill every one of us. But we had too much knowledge of these rascals and their duplicity to be decoyed in that manner, and to trust ourselves to their clemency. We well knew that if we submitted, death would be the inevitable consequence, and therefore preferred risking our chance in the little canoe, as there was a possibility of evading their shot. Immediately turning our boat's head, with our united strength we urged her forward toward the opposite shore. At this instant they commenced a heavy firing at us. Best was soon wounded, and instantly leaped into the water, and clung to the side of the canoe ; Colding also received several wounds, which disabled him from further assistance, so he laid down in the canoe, and Green by his side. All hopes of success seemed now centered in myself; with the rapidity of thought I seized the best paddle, seated myself in the stern of the canoe, and moved her forward with astonishing celerity, reaching in a few minutes the land. Whilst paddling, I felt an acute sensation across the back of my neck and shoulders. On reaching the shore I examined myself, and found that they had put three balls through my clothes, two of which had slightly scarified my flesh. Returning to the ferry we severally recovered from our wounds, but never felt again a disposition to repeat our expedition. Poor Best and Colding had scarcely entered upon duty again before they were both killed by some of these very tories.

On one occasion I was under the necessity of going home on some important business. Soon after my arrival, a company of horse passed directly in front of our residence. My first impression concerning them was that they were a reinforcement of our guard at the ferry. So soon as I had finished my business, I returned with all possible speed, overjoyed at the prospect of an accession to our numbers. On reaching the fort, to my astonishment, I found it completely evacuated. My reinforcement turned out to be a gang of tories from Jackson's Branch, on the Salt-katchie, commanded by that famous old tory, Ned Williams. When they rode up to the ferry, the guard took them to be friends, and gave them a cordial reception, congratulating themselves upon so large an addition to their force. They thus unconsciously and ignorantly delivered themselves up to the enemy, and were taken across the river, and placed in the hands of a large body of British and tories, stationed at Harbard's store, about two miles from the ferry. The intelligence of this capture reached Col. Leroy Hammond (7) at Augusta, who, without delay, marched down at the head of an effective force, and slew nearly the whole of the enemy—releasing and returning with the whig captives to Augusta, from whence my father, who was one among the number taken, came safely home.

The country now seemed to be almost in complete subjugation to the British. Yet had they not been aided and abetted by those unprincipled and blood thirsty tools; those "fiends incarnate, whom it were a base slander to term men;" I say had the tories but shown themselves the genuine sons of America,—the uncompromising, unswerving, champions of liberty, bound together by every social and national tie—the enemy would never have gained a solid foot-hold upon our shores, and tyranny and oppression would sooner have been swept from our land. But how sadly the reverse! They who had grown up "side by side, and hand in hand together," father, son, and brother, were arrayed in mortal and ferocious strife against each other. The friends of liberty were beset on every hand, and from every quarter, until drawn from their homes and families, with stout hearts and strong arms they struck

"For their altars and their fires,
God, and their native land."

Eternal vigilance and action were indispensable, by which, and with a firm reliance on the God of battles they fought, bled, and conquered.

It was seldom indeed that I sought the peaceful shades of my home, as a respite from the laborious duties and toils of the service. The enchantments of the family circle exercise an almost uncontrollable influence over the hearts and minds of men, and yet sweet as are the voices of those we love, and strongly as do cling our heart-strings around the objects of our affections, appealing to our sympathies in loud and soul-stirring language, still louder and more imperative is the call of our country to duty, and the soldier rushes precipitately from the charms and delights of the family circle to the call of his country, his heart burning with patriotic zeal for glory.

Such was the state of things at this crisis, and such was the fire which burned in the breast of every Whig of the Revolution. It was no time for supineness and lamentation—every energy of the soul had to be exercised, for it was the struggle of weakness against strength, of the undisciplined against the disciplined, and of the raw and untutored militia of an infant country, with the well trained regulars of an old, experienced, and skillful nation.

With these truths impressed upon my mind, I allowed myself little or no leisure time, and was either engaged in the performance of duty in the camp, or scouting, as circumstances required. A short time after the capture of our guard at the ferry, I accompanied Col. McCoy, who took command of a small force on a trip to the Ogeechee River, in Georgia, with the view of attacking a little band of tories quartered in that vicinity. These we overtook in the woods, before arriving at the rendezvous; a running fight ensued, but from the denseness of the forest we were thwarted in our design, and the tories made good their escape,—for if my memory serves me correctly, not one of them was killed. Thus frustrated and baffled, we returned to Carolina. On our arrival, we learnt that Capt. James Roberts, who had been scouting with a company on the Edisto River, had (whilst encamping for the night, by some treachery of the tories) been delivered into the hands of Col. Chaney and Williams, who cruelly butchered many of his men, Capt. Roberts and the rest escaping only with their lives. For this outrage we determined to have satisfaction. So thirty-six men, myself among the number, immediately volunteered under Capt. Joseph Vince, a fine officer, and a brave soldier, to pursue these scoundrels, and to avenge the blood of our brave comrades. We overtook some of their number in what is called the "Fork of Edisto River," upon whom we visited summary and immediate justice, killing five or six. From thence we proceeded to Captain Salley's "Cowpens," a few miles distant. Whilst there, our commander rode, unaccompanied, to a mill located near the house of the Pens. Here he was fired upon by several tories lying in ambush hard by, and seriously wounded by musket shot—in consequence of which he was disabled from doing duty for some time. This unfortunate circumstance interrupting our further march, we were compelled to retrace our steps and return to headquarters, Savannah River.

At this time my father's family lived at the Big House, now belonging to Col. Hay, of the Boiling Springs, and a man by the name of Adam Wood lived a near neighbor to them, with whom I formed an acquaintance, and entered into an agreement with, that in the event either of our families were attacked, we should render each other every assistance in our power. But a short time elapsed from the period of the said agreement before a band of tories, passing through that section at night, stopped at Wood's house, killed him, and commenced a general work of destruction, laying waste everything which chanced to be in their way. I distinctly heard the uproar and the firing of arms, and from the direction I knew Wood was attacked. Having retired for the night, I immediately arose, and in company with three others set out for the seat of action. When within a few yards of the house, observing their large and overwhelming numbers, I deemed it prudent to secrete ourselves by the roadside until they had passed. We lay concealed but a few minutes when, having completed their work of death and desolation, the whole party rode by, two deep. As they passed I counted them, and they numbered one hundred and fifty, headed by those notorious scoundrels, robbers, and murderers, who defeated the gallant Roberts on the Edisto, as before stated, Chancy and Williams. They now made their way for the "Big House," but apparently pressed for time, and finding no one at home, (my father's family having taken the precaution during my absence to remove therefrom) they proceeded on their course towards Capt. Vince's station, on Savannah River. Believing that they intended an attack upon the fort, I suggested to John Cave, one of my companions, that we had better set out forthwith, and if possible head them, and apprise Capt. Vince of his danger. So mounting our fleetest horses, we sallied forth with all possible speed, and after considerable difficulty, threading our way through the swamps, we arrived at the fort just before the break of day. I requested the sentinel to inform the captain that I had important intelligence to communicate to him, and desired as quick an interview as possible. The captain returned an answer that he was sick and confined to his bed. I replied that I could take no excuse,—sick or well, he must come out directly. This authoritative command brought him forth immediately. I then related to him what had transpired at the Big House, of the enemy's numbers, and of his approach towards that garrison, advising him, at the same time, to evacuate the fort as soon as possible, unless he felt assured of his safety, and of his being able successfully to contend against so formidable a body, tendering, at the same time, our assistance. He stated to us that his force consisted of but twenty-five men, expressed great doubts of his ability to defend himself against such a numerous enemy, and thought it policy to adopt my suggestion to leave the fort, which was agreed on, and in a few minutes the fort was left to the mercy of the enemy, who in the course of one hour afterwards made a charge upon it with his full force, confidently expecting a prize but instead of a prize they had the sore mortification to find that their deep laid scheme and hellish design on this occasion, was completely baffled.

From this point they turned towards their headquarters, on Edisto. In crossing the Lower Three Runs, they stopped at the house of a Mr. Collins, a very quiet and inoffensive man, and far advanced in years, say about eighty-five. Whatever may have been the sentiments of this old gentleman, he maintained a strictly neutral position, shouldering arms on neither side ; yet those fiends of darkness dispatched him, with his head as white as snow, by the frost of many winters, for an eternal world. How, how could these monsters in human shape dream of prospering, when murdering the aged and inoffensive in this horrid and brutal manner, —and why all this bloodshed ? Because the honest Whigs of the Revolution, knowing full well the rights of man, and daring to maintain them, refused to be galled by the servile chains of a foreign despot, and to bow submissively to his barbarous impositions. It was this which inspired them with invincible fortitude and zeal, and enabled them to throw off the tyrant yoke, and to declare themselves " free, sovereign, and independent."

I continued scouting both in Georgia and Carolina

with very little intermission, until the British, under Sir Henry Clinton, took Charleston, with Gen. Lincoln's army of 4,000 men in 1780,—the intelligence of which threw the whole State into consternation and alarm. Our strong-hold, with the major part of our army, were now effectually in the hands of the enemy, and those poor deluded wretches, the Tories, by this success of their allies at Charleston, seemed urged on with renewed impetuosity in their cruel and diabolical purposes. And dark indeed were the prospects of the friends of liberty about this juncture—despair was depicted in every countenance—our sun became obscured, and seemed ready to go down to rise no more, and the bird of liberty appeared as if taking its parting gaze of the fertile and flowery region over which it had hovered, to plant the tree of liberty—beneath whose bowers the dispersed and oppressed of all nations might find an asylum.

What now to do I knew not. It appeared like madness to remain longer surrounded by an overwhelming foe, liable at any moment to be butchered without mercy, and to flee the country was almost equally trying,—many were pursuing the latter expedient, leaving for other sections, where danger was less threatening and

COLONEL TARLETON

where hostilities had scarcely opened. And my brother, Bartlet Brown, and myself thought it advisable for us to pursue the same course, so we returned to Virginia, our native State. In consequence of the scarcity of clothing during the war, we were poorly clad, and in a bad condition to set out on a journey of 500 miles, and that too with but the paltry sum of three dollars in our pockets to defray expenses. On reaching the "Ridge," about seventy miles from home, our little party had augmented to the number of sixty or seventy, all fleeing the country with the same object in view as ourselves. Journeying onward, we arrived at Fishing Creek, where we encamped a day or two, not wishing to progress too rapidly for fear of overtaking a detachment of British cavalry under Colonel Tarleton, (10) who we learned had been sent by Lord Cornwallis (11) to attack Col. Buford, and had surprised and defeated him at the Waxhaws, (12) and were on their line of march through Charlotte, North Carolina, which lay directly in our route. Whilst encamped at Fishing Creek, a fellow by the name of Mobley, a Tory, came into our camp as a spy. This fellow was so inquisitive, and so particular in examining every body and everything about the premises that our suspicions were very much excited in regard to his true character. We, however, suffered him to depart unmolested. And we afterwards learned that he returned to the encampment, at the head of a large gang of Tories, with a view to capture us, but we anticipated his design, and escaped from his clutches, being at the distance of fifteen or twenty miles when he made his charge upon the tents. Continuing onward, we arrived in sight of Charlotte, when we again encamped, remaining several days. Here many of our party separated from us for different routes, reducing our number to about thirty.

The citizens of Charlotte despatched a messenger to us, praying that in the event the British, who were marching towards that quarter, attacked the town, we would render them assistance. This we promised to do, provided they would furnish us with ammunition, our supply being almost exhausted. On the return of their messenger, they sent us a keg of powder, and lead in proportion. But at the expiration of three days, waiting for the anticipated attack, the citizens of Charlotte informed us that the enemy had gone back. We then " struck our tents" and resumed our march, taking with us the ammunition sent to us by the citizens of Charlotte, which served us in the place of money, as we could barter it for bacon and corn at the mills as we passed on. Throughout the rest of our journey, nothing of importance transpired. We reached our place of destination in Virginia, our mother country, all safe and sound. Shortly after our arrival there, intelligence was received that depredations and outrages, to an alarming extent, had been perpetrated in South Carolina, particularly in our own district. The substance of which was that McGeart (13) and his company of Tories crossed the Savannah River from Georgia, at Summerlin's Ferry, (now called Stone's Ferry), taking the course of the river, and killing every man he met who had not sworn allegiance to the King. This notorious scoundrel passed in this trip through the neighborhood where my father lived, and brutally murdered seventeen of the inhabitants, among whom were my father, Henry Best, and Moore, leaving John Cave for dead, who afterwards recovered. They burnt my father's house level with the ground, and destroyed everything he possessed —my mother and sisters escaping by fleeing to the woods, in which they concealed themselves until the vile wretches departed. But the work of death did not stop here. This atrocious deed of the sanguinary McGeart and his band, was shortly succeeded by another, equally, nay, doubly cruel. The British Colonel Brown (14) marched down from Augusta with an overwhelming force of Tories and Indians, and taking their stand at "Wiggins' Hill," commenced a slaughter of the inhabitants. The news of which reached the ears of those brave and dauntless officers, Cols. McCoy and Harden, who soon hastened to the defence of the terrified Whigs, and coming upon the enemy, charged upon them, and killed and routed them to a man, Col. Brown escaping to the woods. Colonels McCoy and Harden, having accomplished all that was required of them, retired from the field of action, after which, Brown returned with the residue of his force, and retook the "Hill," at which he remained until he hung five of our brave fellows, Britton Williams, Charles Blunt, and Abraham Smith, the names of the other two not recollected,—then he decamped for Augusta. My brother and myself were now in Virginia, among our relations and friends, and would have been as happy as we desired had it not been for the intelligence from South Carolina, particularly of the section we had left. Hearing that the British Tories and Indians had murdered our father, and sixteen more of his neighbors, burning to ashes his house, and all within it, our mother and sisters escaping to the woods, with little or nothing to support upon, and no male friend to help them, my blood boiled within my veins, and my soul thirsted for vengeance. We now learnt that General Washington had sent an army to the South, under the command of Gen. Gates (15) and Baron DeKalb, (16) and we determined forthwith to set out for the seat of strife we had left. In our journey we passed Anson Court House, North Carolina, which we found to be a hot bed of Tories. Col. Wade and his company were stationed there, and the Tories were flocking in and rallying under him from all quarters. On the day of our arrival there, a large gang came in, headed by a fellow who doubtless thought he was doing great things for the King and his servile subjects. My mind could but revolve upon their delusion, and the little value they set upon the rich gems of liberty and independence, with which the Whigs were so enamored, and for which they so hard struggled. It has often been a matter of astonishment to me how we escaped the swarm of Tories at Anson C. H. But so it is, we did, and being eager to accomplish our journey and lose no time, we traveled through long and chilling rains, it being in the fall season, exposing ourselves to imminent danger, for the fever raged with great mortality at that time in that region of country. While at Anson C. H. a fellow endeavored to prevail on us to stay all night with him, but from his suspicious appearance we declined his invitation, and declared our intention to pursue our route, notwithstanding the storm that was then raging. On that night, as well as on several preceding ones, we took shelter under large trees in the swamp, our clothes being as wet as water could make them, and our bodies almost chilled through. In the morning it cleared off, and we pursued our journey.

Overtaking General Marion (17) at "Kingstree," Black River, S. C., we immediately united with his troops. Marion's route lay then between the Santee and Little Pedee Rivers; and being desirous to intercept and defeat Col. Watts, who was then marching at the head of 400 men, between Camden and Georgetown. Every arrangement and preparation was made to carry into execution his design. All things being now ready, Watts appeared in sight at the head of his large force, and as they marched down the road with great show and magnificence, (hoping, no doubt, to terrify and conquer the country) they spied us; at which time, the British horse sallied forth to surround us.

Marion, with his characteristic shrewdness and sagacity, discovered their manœuvres, anticipated their object, and retreated to the woods, some four or five hundred yards, and prepared for them. In a few moments they came dashing up, expecting to find us all in confusion and disorder, but to their astonishment we were ready for the attack, and perceiving this, they called a halt, at which time Marion and Horry ordered a charge. Col. Horry (18) stammered badly, and on this occasion he leaned forward, spurred his horse, waved his sword, and ran fifty or sixty yards, endeavoring to utter the word *charge*, and finding he could not, bawled out, " *damn it, boys, you, you know what I mean, go on.*"

We were then doing what we could, pressing with all rapidity to the strife, and before the British could get back to the main body, we slew a goodly number of them. Being eager to do all the damage we could, we pursued the fellows very close to the line of their main body, and as soon as they got in, Watts began to thunder his cannon at us, and to tear down the limbs and branches of the trees, which fell about us like hail, but did no other damage than to wound one of our men, Natt. Hutson, and one horse slightly. Marion, now finding his force, which consisted only of two hundred men, (though sterling to a man, brave, fearless, and patriotic) was too small to give Watts open battle, guarded the bridges and swamps in his route, and annoyed and killed his men as they passed.

For prudence sake, Marion never encamped over two nights in one place, unless at a safe distance from the enemy. He generally commenced the line of march about sun-set, continuing through the greater part of the night. By this policy he was enabled effectually to defeat the plans of the British and to strengthen his languishing cause. For while the one army was encamping and resting in calm and listless security, not dreaming of danger, the other, taking advantage of opportunity, and advancing through the sable curtains of the night unobserved, often effectually vanquished and routed their foes. It was from the craftiness and ingenuity of Marion, the celerity with which he moved from post to post, that his enemies gave to him the significant appellation of the "Swamp Fox." Upon him depended almost solely the success of the provincial army of South Carolina, and the sequel has proven how well he performed the trust reposed in him. His genuine love of country and liberty, and his unwearied vigilance and invincible fortitude, coupled with the eminent success which attended him through his brilliant career, has endeared him to the hearts of his countrymen, and the memory of his deeds of valor shall never slumber so long as there is a Carolinian to speak his panegyric.

The heavy rains which prevailed at this time, and inundated the country to a considerable extent, proved very favorable to Marion. He now sent a detachment of seventy men, myself one of the number, across the Santee, to attack the enemy stationed at "Scott's Lake" and "Monk's Corner." (19) We crossed the river at night in a small boat, commanded by Captains James and John Postell, dividing our force into two companies, each consisting of thirty-five men. Capt. James Postell took one company and proceeded to "Scott's Lake," but ascertaining the strength of the enemy, and finding the place too well fortified to warrant an attack, he abandoned the project and returned again to the river, and awaited the arrival of Capt. John Postell, who, in the meantime, had marched with the other company to "Monk's Corner." It was my good fortune to accompany the latter. Just about the break of day we charged upon the enemy. Our appearance was so sudden and unexpected that they had not time even to fire a single gun. We took thirty-three prisoners, found twenty odd hogsheads of old spirits, and a large supply of provisions. The former we destroyed, but returned with the latter and our prisoners to the army on Santee. The news of our attack on "Monk's Corner" having reached the enemy at "Scott's Lake," they forthwith marched to their assistance, but arrived too late to extend any :—we had captured their comrades, bursted their hogsheads of spirits, gathered their provisions, and decamped before their arrival. Capt. James Postell, being apprised of their march to assist their friends at "Monk's Corner," returned to the fort, set fire to it, and burned it level to the ground.

Shortly after this circumstance, one of our most efficient officers, Col. Harden, (whom I have before mentioned as having had an important engagement with Brown at "Wiggins' Hill") joined the army under Marion, as also did Major Snipes, who had recently made a miraculous escape from the Tories through the faithfulness of his negro man, Cudjo. Major Snipes related the whole circumstance to me, and displayed the blisters upon his body, occasioned by the intense heat of the flames from the house set on fire by the Tories as he lay concealed in a brier patch close by, a particular account of which may be seen in Horry's life of General Marion (20).

On the first day of April, 1780, I left Gen. Marion on the Big Pedee River, in company with eighty others, forming a detachment under the command of Cols. Harden and Baker, and Major John Cooper. The two last mentioned officers were from Midway settlement, Georgia. There were also several other brave and energetic men, who rendered themselves conspicuous in the war in our detachment, Fountain Stewart, Robert Salley, the Sharps and Goldings from Georgia. Our route lay by the "Four Holes." Crossing the Edisto at Givham's Ferry, we fell in with a man who assisted Brown in hanging the five brave fellows at "Wiggins' Hill." We gave him his due, and left his body at the disposal of the birds and wild beasts. Pursuing our march, we came to "Red Hill," within about two miles of Patterson's Bridge, Saltkatchie. It was now in the night, but the moon being in full strength, and not a cloud to darken her rays, it was almost as bright as day: near this place were stationed a body of Tories, commanded by Capt. Barton. They were desperate fellows, killing, plundering and robbing the inhabitants without mercy or feeling. A company of men, commanded by Major Cooper, were now sent to see what they could do with those murderers. In a few minutes after their departure we heard them fighting, which continued for nearly one hour, when Cooper returned, and told us he had killed the greater part of them, with but the loss of one man, John Steward from Georgia.

We then proceeded on for Pocataligo. Soon after we left Red Hill, we entered upon a long, high causeway; a man came meeting us, and told us Col. Fenwick, with the British horse, were marching on just behind. We paid no attention to him, not knowing who he was, but went ahead; however, we did not go many rods before the advance parties met, and hailed each other—a charge was now ordered on both sides, and we directly came together on the causeway, which was so high that there was no getting off on either side, so a fight was inevitable, and at it we went like bull dogs. The British at length made their way through, though they found it tough work in doing so. We put one of their men to his final sleep on the causeway, and wounded eight more badly, one of whom they had to leave on the road. They wounded one of our men, Capt. James Moore, in thirteen places, though very slightly, and two others who never laid up for their wounds.

We now lay by for two or three days, and then marched for the fort at Pocataligo. When we came in sight of it, I took thirteen of the best mounted men to survey the premises and to lead them out if possible. When we had got within about two hundred yards of Bambifer's house, where the British had deposited their wounded, I saw a negro run in the house, and immediately I saw several men running for the fort—we struck spurs to our horses, and soon came up with them and took them prisoners. When we had gotten them to our company we found them to be Cols. Fennick and Leachmore, (21) who had been out to see their wounded. When we arrived at the fort we had not the smallest hope of taking it, but now finding we had two of their most efficient officers, [Major Andrew Devo (22) the only one in the fort] Colonels Harden and Baker sent a flag in for them to give up the fort. When the flag was passing by Col. Fennick, he asked what that meant. On being told it was for them to surrender the fort, he ripped and swore, and hoped "that if they did surrender it, they might all be in hell before the morrow."

After deliberation in the fort for the space of two hours, they all marched out, well armed, tied their horses to what was then called "Abatis," advanced some little distance from the fort, and formed a line. We then marched between them and the fort and took them prisoners,—they having one hundred and ten men, and we eighty. If all the men in the fort had been brave and true to their cause, I don't think one thousand men could have taken them, for the fort was advantageously located and well fortified, approachable only at three points, all of which were well guarded by a deep creek and cannons. Part of the men in the fort were as good Whigs as we had—Col. Stafford, Col. Davis, Capts. Felts and Green, whose son was with us, also others. We now paroled the prisoners and sent them to Charleston, then burnt the house and leveled the fort with the ground. Next day Col. McCoy, who had been out-laying, came down to us, and my brother Bartlett and myself left Col. Harden and came off with him. On our way we called in at old Mr. Hext, at Coosawhatchie, the father of the late Lawrence Hext, of the Boiling Springs, Beaufort District. After we left Mr. Hext's, and had progressed some distance, a young man behind us, named Wald, whose horse was jaded and traveled slowly, met Ned Williams, with a gang of Tories, who asked him who those were that turned up the lane. He told them that it was Col. McCoy and his company, and that the fort at Pocataligo was taken. They then broke for the Saltkatchie. Wald now came up and told us the circumstance, and we immediately pushed after them, and followed them into the Saltkatchie swamp, but could not overtake them. We returned, got dinner, and encamped that night near the water pond, on the side next to Capt. John Cater's Boiling Springs, in a pine thicket, a little below the Springs. Next morning we went up to the "Big House," now belonging to Col. Hay, and there found those of my father's family that the Tories and Indians had left, whom we had not seen before for twelve months. To describe the joy of that meeting is inexpressible :—we now beheld some of those, who were endeared to us by the strongest ties of nature, whom we never expected to see again this side of eternity's ocean, thinking they had fallen victims to the awful storm of war which had been and was then raging. Here we could have remained with them, and gladly toiled and labored for their comfort and happiness, but such was our country's great demand for services, we could only stay a few moments with them.

Bidding them farewell, with no hope of meeting them again, we marched for the siege of Augusta. On our way up we learned that Col. Brown's (a Tory) boats were going up the Savannah River. We went in pursuit of them, and attacked them about opposite the place of the late Stephen Smith, of Savannah River, but they got on the Georgia side, and we could do nothing with them. From this we marched to Augusta, where we met Generals Pinckney and Twiggs, and commenced the work of extermination. The first attack we made was on the fort at Silver Bluff, (23) now the property of Gov. Hammond, of South Carolina. Brown's boats had now arrived, and stowed away their goods in the fort. The British not being willing to yield without a struggle, we stove a cannon ball through the brick house in the fort, and they immediately marched out and surrendered, for fear we would serve them the like trick.

The next fort we attacked was that commanded by the wretched Grason, at the upper end of the town. This we soon stormed and took—Capt. Alexander shooting Grason for his villainous conduct in the country. Some made their escape from us by fleeing to Brown's fort near the river. Before we laid siege to Brown's fort, a fellow by the name of Rutherford (a villain withal) took a company and slipped out in the night down the river, opposite Beech Island, (24) and just at the break of day, surprised our horse-guard. It being in the bend of the river, the British and Tories got round them, and having a superior force, our men took to the river, but they killed several of our brave fellows while they were swimming, some making their escape—my brother, Bartlett Brown, was one among that number. We heard of their trip after our guard and pushed to cut them off, but were too late by a few moments only, for as we got within one hundred and fifty yards of the lane, we saw them enter. A few moments sooner, and we would have fixed them snugly.

We now commenced the siege of Brown's fort. In taking this fort we had great difficulty. We raised a platform fifteen or twenty feet high, and mounted a cannon upon it, and from thence fired at them in the fort. In this way we destroyed a good many of them, but finding we were too hard for them in this way, and to screen themselves from the thunder and lightning of our platform, they dug caves in the sides of the walls of the fort and crawled into them. We then continued the entrenchment, and as we entrenched, we rolled up cowhides and placed them on the embankment for portholes to shoot through. One morning I was standing next to young Stafford, who was about to shoot through one of our-port holes, and there came a ball from the fort and killed him dead. Young Stafford was with me in Gen. Marion's army, and he was, indeed, a brave and patriotic fellow, and dying in freedom's cause, his memory should never fade from our recollection. Before Brown would surrender, we entrenched so near his fort that I could run a hoe-helve from the entrenchment into the fort. On finding we were so near upon him, he marched out and surrendered with all his force and goods. Brown had been such a desperate fellow, there existed great anxiety to kill him ; but as he came under the capitulation, we had no chance to do so at this time, but I determined to do so on his way down the river. I took a few brave fellows, and slipped down the river to carry into execution my determination, but he made his escape, through the shades of the night, in a small canoe.

When we commenced the siege of Augusta, it was the first of April, 1781 ; when we closed, it was the first of the ensuing August. Having labored so hard and incessantly to dig Brown out of his fort, I concluded when I had done so to take a peep into it, but it was a sore peep to me, as I took the small-pox from it.

I now went home very sick, and as none of our family had ever had it, I had to take the woods—so I retreated back of the Big House to an old field, next to the swamp, under a large oak tree. The weather being very hot, I suffered intensely. While there I employed one Peggy Ogleby to be my nurse. This slut was a Tory, and informed her clan where I was. They said they would come and kill the d—n rebel, but as I had an invisible and Almighty Protector, they had not the power to execute their malicious design. If I am not mistaken, the period I lay under that oak was forty days. When I recovered, I joined Major Cooper, at Beech Island, and we continued scouting until the end of the war, in December, 1782. I then returned home, but the British and Tories had nearly destroyed everything we possessed. My mother lived but a short time after the close of the war, and the estate she left each child, was thirty-nine pounds, ten shillings sterling.

Although the war had closed, the Tories were still troublesome, plundering and occasionally killing the inhabitants. The foremost scoundrels in this diabolical work, were John Black, Zekiel Maulfers, Lark Loudon, and two others, whose names I will not mention, as they have relations in the country who could not help what they did. These fellows murdered a good man at Cherry Hill, Ga.; for which, John Black and the two whose names are not mentioned, were killed and hung at Savannah;—the other two, the worst of the clan, made their escape to Carolina, where they murdered and plundered until the citizens were afraid to travel the roads, day or night. Finding the Whigs were upon the look out for them, they stole Judge Haywood's match horses, and five negroes, and horses from various persons, and started for the Western country.

I heard of their crossing the ridge, and being unwilling they should escape with impunity, I got three other men, Richard Simmons, Gill Thomas, and Benjamin Brown, and put out after them. We pursued them into East Tennessee—over Watorger, we came upon them and took them prisoners. It was now in the month of January, and extremely cold; the snow was on the ground two feet deep, and withal, I had the meazles very badly. What to do I hardly knew. I concluded, however, to risk the consequences, and bidding farewell to these cold and frozen regions, I began to retrace my steps with my prisoners and their plunder. We crossed the Watorger on the ice, and when we had gotten on the Yellow Mountains it snowed again and freezed on the top, so that a passage through it was very difficult. We had to force our way by changing the foremost horse every hundred yards. Just as we got to the turn in the mountain, night overtook us, so we encamped for the night, building our fire out of the chestnut limbs on the snow. Next morning we came down to the foot of the mountains, to one Samuel Bright, and got a little dry pumpkin for our breakfast, the people having little or nothing else to eat. Having so many prisoners, horses, and negroes, our funds now run out, so we had to sell what we could spare to defray expenses. We now came to Pad. Bryant's, where these runaways had left one of Judge Haywood's horses, which we got, and tarried all night. It was indeed a dark and rainy night, and the prisoners thought to take an advantage of us by it, so they framed an excuse to go out. Being handcuffed and tied, I apprehended no danger, but I took one of my company along with me. They had, unperceived, loosed the rope under their blankets. It was in an old field, on the slant of a hill, and when we had gotten out, they started to run down the hill. My gun being loaded with buck-shot, I fired at one of them, and stuck one shot in his ancle, his foot being up at the crack of the gun, the shot run up into the calf of his leg, but it did not bring him to the ground. Being young and active, I now threw down my gun and pushed after him, and just as I was about to take hold of him I struck a stump, which knocked me over, but I soon recovered from my fall, and put out after him again ; and as before, just as I was about to take him the second time, I ran upon the second stump, which threw me clean over. I now gave up the chase, as by this time he had gotten too far. Next morning I had a curiosity to examine the ground I had run over after these fellows, and I found but the single two stumps in the way—they had just missed them, and I run over both. We now went in pursuit of these villains, when we soon came upon one, and in taking him, Simmons, put an end to his existence ; the other was taken the next day, and put in the 96th District prison. When we had gotten home, we sent for him, and he was carried to Beaufort, where there were seven indictments against him. He was tried, condemned and hung. On the delivery of Judge Haywood's horses to him, he gave me twenty-five guineas, not only for his horses, but also for putting a stop to the outrages of these villains. The other persons whose property we brought back, gave us five guineas apiece, and the public gave us twenty-five pounds sterling.

Some time after the close of these things, I married and settled myself between the Sand Hill and Cedar branches, waters of the Lower Three Runs, Barnwell district. On each of these streams I built mills, and from the mills, between which I lived, I gave my place the name of "Fork Mills." The mills are now owned by Major William H. Peyton, my son-in-law. From this place I moved to Boiling Springs, where I have lived and enjoyed fine health for many years, and where I expect to die, if I die at home. I have followed the delightful business of farming ever since the close of the war, and the Lord has been pleased to grant me enough of the good things of this life to keep me free from want down to the present moment.

NOTES.

(1) GEN. STEPHEN BULL, of Beaufort, S. C., was Colonel of one of the regiments first raised by South Carolina, and supported the Georgians when struggling to escape the Royal Government. His brother, William Bull, was a physician by profession, and was Royal Governor of South Carolina for many years. Though he was firm in his allegiance to the King, he exercised his office with great dignity and propriety, and was in fact a great favorite in his State.

(2) COL. WILLIAM HARDEN, was a native of Barnwell District, S. C. He was first appointed captain of the Beaufort Artillery by the council of safety, about the middle of March, 1776. He was placed in command of Fort Littleton, opposite the town of Beaufort, where he remained about fourteen months. He then become Colonel of militia, in Beaufort and Barnwell Districts, and continued in active service on the southern frontier of South Carolina, and occasionally on the Georgia side of the river.

(3) SIR HENRY CLINTON was the grandson of Francis, sixth

Earl of Lincoln. After distinguishing himself in the battle of Bunker Hill, in 1775, he was sent unsuccessfully against New York and Charleston. He afterwards, in Sept., 1776, occupied the city of New York. On the 6th October, 1777, he assaulted and took forts Clinton and Montgomery. In 1778 he succeeded Gen. Howe in the command at Philadelphia, whence Washington compelled him to retire. In May. 1780, he took Charleston, for which he received the thanks of the House of Commons. It was he who negotiated with Arnold in his treason. He returned to England in 1782, where he published a narrative of his conduct in America, 1782, observations on Cornwallis' answer, 1783, and observations on Stedman, 1784. He was made Governor of Gibraltar a few months before his death. He died Dec. 22d, 1795.

(4) ADMIRAL MARRIOT ARBUTHNOT, was the son of the celebrated Dr. Arbuthnot, the distinguished friend of Pope and Swift. He was made a lieutenant of the navy in August, 1739, and in 1746 commanded the Jamaica sloop, with the rank of master and commander. In April, 1747, the Jamaica, in company with the Surprise, of twenty guns, took the Superbe, a French ship of thirty-six guns and 136 men, designed for the South Sea, and valued at £70,000. In June, 1747, he was made a post-captain. On the breaking out of the Revolution, he was appointed commissioner of the navy yard at Halifax, in Nova Scotia, and soon after he was raised to the rank of Admiral, and also made Governor of Nova Scotia. In 1779 he was appointed to the command of the fleet in North America. On his arrival in New York, he acted with great spirit and humanity, in rectifying the enormous abuses of the Naval Hospital on Long Island. About the 1st Dec., he convoyed Sir Henry Clinton and part of his army to Charleston, and commanded the fleet at that place upon its capitulation.

(5) GEN. ANDREW PICKENS, was born in Paxton Township, Penn., on the 19th Sept. 1739, and was of French descent. In 1752 his father removed from Virginia, where he had resided for a few years, and settled in Waxhaw, S. C. Andrew served in the French war, which terminated in 1763, and he then began to develop those qualities for which he was afterwards so celebrated. At the commencement of the Revolution, he raised a military company, and was appointed the captain. He acted a distinguished part throughout the struggle for independence, and his zeal, skill, and courage were rewarded by his country, in his being rapidly promoted to the respective commands of Major, Colonel, and Brig.-Gen. In the year 1782, he commanded in chief an expedition against the Cherochee Indians. He was with Gen. Lincoln at the battle of Stono, and had his horse killed under him, while covering the retreat ordered by that General. At the battle of Cowpens, he commanded the militia forces, and for his gallantry and bravery on that occasion, Congress voted him a sword. He was possessed of great sagacity and decision, collected courage and prudence with sleepless watchfulness. At the close of the war he served in various civil capacities. He died suddenly at Tumassee, Pendleton District, S. C., in the year 1817, apparently in full health, at the age of 78 years.

(6) SISTERS' FERRY,—a village in South Carolina, twenty-five miles from Coosawatchie, and one hundred and three miles from Charleston.

(7) BENJAMIN LINCOLN was born in Hingham, Mass., Jan. 23d, 1733. His advantages for education were limited, and until the age of forty he was employed in the pursuits of agriculture. He was appointed in Feb., 1776, a Brigadier, and soon after a Maj.-Gen., in the Provincial army, and in Feb., 1777, a Maj.-Gen. on

the Continental establishment. His services were conspicuous towards the close of that year, in the Northern Campaign. He was second in command in the army which, under Gen. Gates, captured the British under Burgoyne. On the day after the battle of Stillwater, he received a dangerous wound while reconnoitering. In the following year, he was appointed by Congress to take command in the Southern department, at the solicitation of the delegates from that portion of the Union. After a number of inferior operations, on the 20th of June, 1779, he made an unsuccessful attack on the British post at Stono Ferry. He afterwards retired to Charleston, and attempted its defence, but was compelled on the 12th May, 1780, to capitulate. He was exchanged in November, and in the spring following, he joined the army on the North River. At the siege of Yorktown, he commanded a central division, and shared largely in the dangers and triumphs of the day. He was designated to conduct the surrendering army to the field, where their arms were deposited, and to see the conditions of the capitulation executed. In Oct., 1781, he became Secretary of the War Department, and after the establishment of peace he returned to his native State, and in 1787 was appointed to command the troops engaged in suppressing the insurrection in Massachusetts. In 1788 he was chosen Lieutenant-Governor of Massachusetts, and he afterwards held the office of collector of the ports of Boston and Charlestown. He died in the house in which he was born, on the 9th day of May, 1810, aged 78 years.

(8) BRIER'S CREEK.—At this place Gen. Ashe, with 1500 North Carolina militia and a few regular troops, was on the 3d day of March, 1779, surprised by Col. Prevost, who, taking a circuitous route, came upon his rear with 900 men. The militia were thrown into confusion and fled at the first fire. The Americans

had 150 killed and as many taken prisoners. The whole artillery, stores, baggage, and nearly all the arms were captured by the enemy. A few Continentals, under Elbert, made a brave resistance, but the survivors of this body, with their gallant leader, were at last compelled to surrender.

(9) COL. LE ROY HAMMOND, was born in Richmond Co., Va. He left Virginia about 1765, and became a merchant in Augusta, Georgia. He afterwards removed to South Carolina, where he continued the mercantile business for a while, and then became an extensive cultivator of tobacco. He took an active part in the Revolution, and rendered conspicuous services to his country. He was engaged in the battle of Stono, and at the siege of Ninety-Six. He was distinguished for his bravery and gallantry. He died in Edgefield District, S. C., leaving but one descendant.

(10) COL. BANASTER TARLETON was born in Liverpool, in 1754, and was the son of a merchant of eminence in that place. He was intended for the counting house, but having no relish therefor, he entered the army as a cornet of dragoons, about the beginning of the Revolution. He soon embarked for America as a volunteer, and after his arrival, Sir William Erskine, of the cavalry, noticing his spirit, vigor, and capacity, appointed him his Brigade-Major. In this situation he acted in 1777, and part of 1778, with the main army in Pennsylvania. As Gen. Howe seldom, if ever, brought his cavalry to serious action, Tarleton had no opportunity of displaying his character. He had plenty of time for frolic, and when he was not riding races on the common against Major Gwynne, he was making love to the ladies, and indulging in every sort of excess. At one time he was fairly caught " in flagrante delicto," with Major Crew's mistress. In 1778 he became Lieutenant-Colonel of the British Legion, a

corps which had just been raised. In his campaign in the South he distinguished himself for his activity, his bravery, and his cruelty. After the war he returned to England. He subsequently became General Tarleton, and was M.P. for Liverpool and Governor of Berwick. He died at Leintwardine Co., Salop, in the year 1833, aged 79 years.

(11) LORD CHARLES CORNWALLIS was born on the 31st Dec.. 1738. His title, as eldest son of Earl Cornwallis, was Lord Viscount Broome. He was appointed, August 4th, 1759, Capt. in Crawford's Royal Volunteers, and on May 1st, 1761, Lieut.-Col. of the 12th Regt. On the 25th of the same month he joined his regiment in Germany, where he served with distinction. In July, 1765, he was made Lord of the Bed Chamber, and in August 2d, Aid-de-Camp to the King, with the rank of Col., and in March, 1766, he was appointed Col. of the 33d Regt. On the 14th July, 1768, he was married to Miss Jemima Jones, a lady of most excellent disposition, and large fortune, and niece of Lt.-Gen. Daniel Jones, of the 2d Regt. In Dec., 1770, he was made constable of the Tower, and in Sept. 29, 1775, was raised to the rank of Maj.-Gen. In 1776 he embarked for America, with his own and five other regiments. He distinguished himself at the battle of Long Island, and at Fort Washington he supported the second·column in their attack on that place, at the head of the Grenadiers and the 33d Regt. Lady Cornwallis being in declining health, he was about to embark for England, after his return to New York, but on hearing the result of the battle of Trenton, his zeal for his King superseded all family considerations, however dear to his heart, and he instantly left New York and rejoined the army. He distinguished himself greatly during the war, and was promoted to the rank of Lieut.-Gen. He defeated Gates at Camden, with a much inferior force, and reduced South

Carolina to subjection, but these advantages were tarnished by the surrender of his army at Yorktown, in 1781—an event which established the independence of America. He was, notwithstanding, never blamed for want of courage, prudence, or sagacity, but on the contrary, the gallant conduct and high military talents he had at all times shown, recommended him to the Ministry, and he accordingly became Governor-General of India, where he regained his laurels in the defeat of Tippoo, whom he compelled to sue for peace. He afterwards became Lord-Lieutenant of Ireland, and subsequently became again Governor of India. He died Oct. 5th, 1805, leaving one son and one daughter surviving him. His remains were interred at Glazepore, with every mark of honor and respect. His wife died in 1779, while he was in America.

(12) The engagement at the Waxhaws occurred on the 29th day of May, 1780. The Americans were composed of some Virginia troops, under the command of Col. Buford. Confiding in their distance from the enemy, they had been at no pains to choose a proper position. Cornwallis, having been apprised of their situation, detached Col. Tarleton, with 700 light cavalry and a new corps of infantry called the Legion, mounted on horseback, to rout and disperse them, before they could be reinforced. By pushing on with unexampled celerity, Tarleton came upon the Americans suddenly and unexpectedly, and after a short encounter, routed the party, and captured the artillery, baggage, colors, and indeed everything. The carnage was terrible The Americans, inferior in number, made but a feeble resistance, and cried for quarter. This was refused, and the infuriated enemy continued to cut down and massacre them without mercy, until satiated and tired with slaughter. The Americans had 108 killed, and 150 wounded, and 53 taken prisoners, while the loss of the

British was only 7 killed and 12 wounded. "Tarleton's Quarters" became afterwards a by-word to express deliberate cruelty.

A particular account of Col. Buford's defeat is contained in Garden's Anecdotes of the Revolution, 2d series, p. 135.

' (13) DANIEL MACGIRTH was a native of Kershaw District, South Carolina. He at first took sides with the Americans, and rendered valuable services to his country. Having committed a breach of subordination, which could not be overlooked in an army, he was tried by a court martial, and sentenced to be publicly whipped. He then vowed vengeance against the American cause, and afterwards executed his threats most fearfully and vindictively, causing much public and private suffering. When the Americans recovered the State he fled into Georgia, and thence into Florida. When Florida was reconveyed to the Spaniards, by the treaty of peace, he became subject to their laws or suspicions, and was arrested and confined by them for five years, in one of their damp dungeons in the castle of St. Augustine, where his health was totally destroyed. He died in misery, but not in want. The father of MacGirth was a captain in the South Carolina militia at the time of his son's defection, but continued firmly and devotedly attached to the interests of his country.

(14) COL. THOMAS BROWNE, of Augusta, Geo., commanded a body of Royalists and Indians, and committed many aggressions upon the inhabitants of South Carolina during the revolution, butchering peaceful citizens, and destroying their houses, cattle, and provisions.

(15) GEN. HORATIO GATES was born in England, in 1728. In early life he entered the British navy. He was aid to Gen. Monckton at the capture of Martinico, and was at the defeat

of Gen. Braddock, in 1755, where he was shot through the body. At the commencement of the Revolution, he was appointed by Congress Adjutant-General, with the rank of Brigadier-General. In June, 1776, he was appointed to the command of the army of Canada, but was superseded by Gen. Schuyler in May, 1777. In August following he took the place of this officer in the Northern Department. The success which attended his arms in the capture of Burgoyne filled America with joy. Congress passed a vote of thanks, and ordered a gold medal to be presented to him by the President, in honor of this event. It should be mentioned here, however, that most of the credit of this achievement properly belongs to Generals Arnold and Morgan, who were the real actors in the affair, and without the aid of whose services, a different result altogether might have been produced. In June, 1780, Gates was transferred to the command of the Southern Department, and in August following, he was totally defeated and routed by Cornwallis, with an inferior force, at Camden, S. C. His conduct in that engagement proves him, as a military man, to have been of but very ordinary ability. In fact, to sum up his character, he was a vain, conceited man, puffed up with the idea of his own consequence, flattered by attention, and perfectly intoxicated by success. Such was the man who attempted to supplant the immortal Washington!!! After the peace, Gates retired to his farm in Berkeley, Va., where he remained until 1780, when he moved to the city of New-York, where he died on the 10th day of April, 1806, aged 77.

(16) BARON DE KALB was a native of Germany, and was born about the year 1717. He came to America with Lafayette, in 1777, and on the 15th September following, was commissioned a Major-General by Congress. When Lincoln's overthrow at Charleston opened the South to the British, he was sent with

2,000 Continentals to operate against them, and had he been left alone, would have given a good account of himself, as he was a brave, experienced, and able officer. But Congress appointed Gen. Gates, a vain and fool-hardy man, to the command of the South, and thereby changed the whole aspect of affairs, and in the battle of Camden the American army was totally defeated, by an inferior force under Cornwallis. The militia gave way at once, and fled in the utmost confusion, Gates following after them with full speed, leaving poor De Kalb with his Continentals to fight the battle as best they could. The Continentals were cut to pieces in endeavoring to save the main army, and the noble De Kalb fell, pierced with eleven wounds, and died August 16th, 1780.

It is singular that Congress, so discreet in awarding medals to the heroes of Saratoga, did not present a similar gift to Gates for the part he took at Camden. The celerity of his flight to Charlotte on that occasion has never been equalled in ancient or modern times, not even by John Gilpin himself. It was a common report that day, that he killed three horses in his eighty mile ride.

(17) FRANCIS MARION was born at Winyaw, near Georgetown S. C., in the year 1732. In 1759 he served as a soldier against the Cherochee Indians. At the commencement of the revolution he was appointed captain in the regiment of Col. Moultrie. He soon after received a Major's commission, and assisted at the defence of Sullivan's Island in 1776. Being promoted to a lieutenant-colonelcy, he was intrusted with a small corps employed in harassing the British and Tories, and gained a number of important advantages, which procured him, in 1780, the commission of Brigadier-General. He continually surprised and captured parties of the British and their friends by the secrecy

and rapidity of his movements. In 1780 his troops, which had amounted to only a few hundred, and often to only a few dozen were reinforced by the legion of Gen. Lee, and he soon after captured a number of forts, and forced the British to retire to Charleston. He joined the main army under Gen. Green a short time before the battle of Eutaw Springs, and received the thanks of Congress for his intrepid conduct in that action. After the British evacuated Charleston, he retired to his plantation, and soon after married Mary Videau, a lady of wealth. He represented his parish of St. John's in the Senate of the State, and in May, 1790, was a member of the convention for forming the State Constitution. He was one of the ablest partisan officers of the Revolution, and one of the most successful. He seldom failed of capturing his enemy, and almost always did it by surprise. His courage was the boldest, his movements the most rapid, his discipline severe, and his humanity most exemplary. He died on the 27th day of February, 1795, aged 63 years.

(18) COL. PETER HORRY was a descendant of one of the many Protestant families who moved to Carolina from France, after the revocation of the Edict of Nantz. He early took up arms in defence of his country, and through all the trials of peril and privation experienced by Marion's brigade, gave ample proof of his strict integrity and undaunted courage. The fame which he acquired, as one of the band of heroes who defended the post at Sullivan's Island, was never tarnished. No man more eagerly sought the foe, none braved danger with greater intrepidity. He was a brother of Col. Hugh Horry, who was also a very able officer.

(19) MONK'S CORNER was, before the Revolution, a place of some commercial importance. There were three or four well

kept taverns and five or six excellent stores there. These last were generally branches of larger establishments in Charleston, and as they sold goods at Charleston prices, they commanded a fair business. The usual practice of the Santee planter was to take his crop to Monk's Corner, sell it there, receiving cash or goods in exchange, dine, and return home in the afternoon. A party of American cavalry were stationed near this place during the Revolution. On the night of 14th August, 1780, they were surprised by a party of British under command of Col. Tarleton, and completely routed and dispersed. On another occasion, the Americans surprised a party of British here.

(20) MAJOR SNIPES was a Carolinian, of remarkable strength and courage, and a vindictive hater of the Tories. He had suffered some injuries at their hands, which he never forgave. His sanguinary temper led him to treat them with such ferocity that he was more than once subject to the harshest rebuke of his commander. On one occasion he had leave of absence for awhile, and repaired to his plantation. The Tories fell upon his trail, and followed him. Unconscious of pursuit, and lulled into security by the apparent silence of the neighborhood, he retired to rest, and fatigued with the labors of the day soon fell into a profound sleep. At midnight he was aroused by the cries of his faithful negro, Cudjo, and apprised of the approach of the Tories, who were already on the plantation. Snipes at once started up, and proposed to shelter himself in the barn, but he was told that it was in flames. He then rushed forth, covered only by his night-shirt, and flew, by the advice of his negro, to a thick copse of briars and brambles, within fifty yards of his dwelling, and hid himself. Though his shirt was torn from his back by the briars, and his flesh lacerated by them, yet once there, he lay effectually concealed. The Tories, in the meantime,

surrounded the house. Fearing the arm of Snipes, and knowing his courage, they dared not enter the dwelling, but set it on fire, and with pointed muskets waited for him to emerge. The house was consumed, and the intense heat of the flames drew blisters upon the body of poor Snipes, who nevertheless bore it all with the most manly fortitude. Finding themselves foiled in their object, the Tories then seized the negro, and threatened him with instant death unless he revealed the hiding place of his master. But the courage and fidelity of the negro was superior to the terror of death. Though a rope was placed around his neck, and he was thrice run up the tree to which it was fixed, and choked nearly to strangulation, yet he still refused to disclose the secret. His capacity to endure proved superior to the will of the Tories to inflict, and he was at length cut down, and left on the ground half dead. While this was going on, Snipes was but a few steps from them, and heard their threats, beheld all their proceedings, and witnessed the bravery and fidelity of his slave. Snipes and Cudjo had been brought up together from childhood, had played, fished, and hunted together, and were mutually attached to each other, and the noble-hearted slave truly bore for his master " that love which is stronger than death."

(21) COL. LECHMERE commanded Fort Balcour. He was at one time taken prisoner. He was the brother-in-law of Colonel Deveaux.

(22) COL. ANDREW DEVEAUX was descended from a Huguenot family, which settled in Beaufort District, after the repeal of the Edict of Nantz. He was remarkable from childhood for mischief, bravery and adventure. He took sides with the British, and being a man of considerable military genius, was of the utmost value to them. After the war, he married Miss Ver-

planck, of New-York, and lived at an elegant country-seat on the Hudson River. He had two daughters, one of whom married Col. Hare Powell, of Philadelphia. He was fond of gaiety and display. He drove his own carriage with four elegant horses about the streets of New-York, wearing an ostrich feather in his hat, at a time when such decorations were unknown, even among the gay of that city. Through his extravagance, he consequently outlived his fortune, and became embarrassed before his death.

(23) SILVER BLUFF.—A British post was established here in the Revolution, called Fort Dreadnaught. On the 21st day of May, 1781, it was surrendered to a detachment of Lee's Legion, commanded by Capt. Rudolph. One field piece and a considerable supply of stores were captured, besides some prisoners.

(24) BEECH ISLAND derives its name from the number of beech trees which grow upon it.

www.ingramcontent.com/pod-product-compliance
Lightning Source LLC
Chambersburg PA
CBHW020246090426
42735CB00010B/1859